Spells

"If this be magic, let it be an art
Lawful as eating."

William Shakespeare
The Winters Tale
Act V, Scene III

Spells

Spellcraft to bring magic to your life
and reality to your desires

Matthew Green

PARKGATE
BOOKS

Contents

Contents

introduction

Since the earliest days of the earthly existence of human beings ordinary people from all parts of the globe have performed acts of magic to keep their lives running smoothly. There are literally countless spells both recorded on paper and passed down by word of mouth that seek to benefit the user by attracting love, warding away negativity, averting disaster, improving finances, protecting the self, their children and loved ones from harm. And there are spells to give thanks to the earth for providing humanity with their basic needs: food, the warmth of the sun and the love of one's kindred.

The vast body of spells handed down through the generations revolve around the manipulation of symbolic objects empowered by will to achieve a desired end. This type of enchantment is referred to as "sympathetic" magic because it uses a symbol to represent something (a person or thing) and another symbol or symbols to act upon it, representing the desired outcome.

For example, candles may be used to represent a desired lover by being rubbed with sweet smelling oils and lit while the spellcaster visualizes him or herself and the desired lover in a passionate embrace — the intention here is that the person represented by the candle will feel an irresistible attraction to the spellcaster. The magic is sympathetic in that a familiarity between the symbol (in this case the candle) and the love object is forged and acted upon (sweetness of oil and heat of flame) within the mind of the conjurer.

Another type of magic often encountered in spellcrafting may be referred to as "empathic" where a part of an object stands for the whole. For example, the use of a person's signature, hair or an article of clothing is used to represent that person. The basis of this belief is that a potent psychic bond exists between something taken from a person and the person from whom the item is taken. Magic performed on the object is believed to cross this psychic bridge acting directly upon that person.

Spells are largely driven by the use of traditional symbols such as herbs, candles and perfumes. In folk magic none of the tools used were ever expensive or difficult to obtain. Folk magicians used what was readily available and if a particular herb, root or flower was out of season, another related herb was used instead.

Spellcrafting is a highly individual process of interaction with other people and the earth on a deeply spiritual level.

The spells and charms in this book use readily available ingredients and tools found at home — herbs, candles, needles, thread, crystals and other things you may already have. A lot of space, time or money is unnecessary in creating some very powerful spells. But you must have faith in yourself and a deep inner belief you can attain your desired end.

Negative spells and dark magical practices are largely the fabrication of fictional books and movies and serve no real purpose in the lives of sane and positive people. There is never a valid reason to curse another person because negativity can only beget negativity.

Within these pages are spells from all over the earth, from both the ancient and modern worlds. The Caribbean provides a vast treasury of spells many of which are included as are several from America's South, Europe, Native American cultures and Brazil.

Enjoy being creative with your spellcrafting. Experimentation with different spells will lead you to discover those that work best for you.

As you develop your intuition you will find you automatically use certain types of herbs and oils in your own tailormade spells. It is then you will weave the most potent magic.

The Craft of Spells

Spells are highly creative mini rituals which make use of items found in nature and the material world such as herbs, crystals, oils, candles and flowers. The list that follows shows the types of items used within the spells in this book. You will not have to look far for most of the spices, flowers and candles used, nor will you need to spend a lot of money. In fact chances are you have many of the ingredients about your home, waiting to become part of your enchantments.

Magical Tools used in Spellcasting

Candles and Oil Lamps

Tapers of many different hues are used in spellcasting and whenever possible it is always preferable, but not essential, to use natural candles. Beeswax or those made with vegetable fat are best of all, although many successful spells make use of paraffin candles.

Occasionally spells may call for the use of an oil-burning lamp. In this case use the safest type available. Quality lamp oil, suitable for your chosen lamp, should be used as the base oil to which you add other essential oils and perfumes.

Cloth, Pins and Needles

Cloths such as wool, cotton and flannel are used to make charm bags. Silks, velvets, linens and homespun cotton may also be used to good effect. When spell materials are to be wrapped in a cloth of a particular color at the conclusion of a spell, silk is believed to be the best choice as it is considered to have qualities that insulate magic.

Pins and needles are also used in spells where they may be pushed into candles or charms as a symbolic mark of an intention.

Unless you are directed otherwise always use brand new needles and pins.

Crystals and Minerals

Most people are aware of the healing powers of crystals though many do not realize they can be used to great effect in spells. Crystals such as citrine, rose quartz, iron pyrites, amethyst, amber and lodestone are frequently employed in spells as are other minerals such as magnets and iron filings.

Bottles and Jars

Many Caribbean spells use jars and bottles as active parts of spells and they can also be used to store magical oils and powders.

It is best to store magical blends of essential oils in dark glass bottles — this prevents light touching the blend which causes it to become rancid.

There are oil bottles on the market of so many different colors that blends may be stored in bottles appropriately colored for the purpose. Oils for love could be stored in pink or red bottles, prosperity oils in green, luck and success formulas in yellow, and purifying, protecting and exorcizing oils in purple colored bottles.

Perfumes, Oils and Powders

Quite a few spells call for mixtures of powdered herbs and essential oils which can be made according to the recipes in these pages. Perfumes and aftershave lotions are used in many spells to sweeten an individual's disposition or to anoint charm bags and amulets.

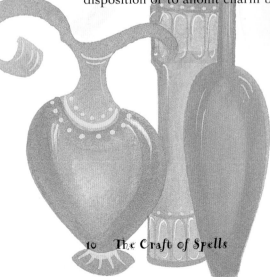

The Astrological Planets and their Days

A great number of spells are timed for performance on particular days of the week. This is because each of the seven days in the week are ruled by one of five planets or the Sun or Moon and each of these planets rule over a different facet of human endeavor. Below is a list of the planets, their powers and days. Spellcasters should refer to the chart to time their spells for maximum effect.

Planet	Day	Powers
The Sun	Sunday	Glory, majesty, social and political advancement. The magic of fatherhood.
The Moon	Monday	Secrecy, mystery, peace and the magic of pregnancy. The magic of motherhood.
Mars	Tuesday	Force, mastery, power and the magic of protection.
Mercury	Wednesday	Luck, psychic work, communication and attracting customers.
Jupiter	Thursday	Prosperity, wealth, success and work.
Venus	Friday	Love, attraction, friendship and the performance of Caribbean wealth spells.
Saturn	Saturday	Wisdom, restrictive magic, breaking bad habits and stopping others harassing you.

Herbs

Herbs used in cooking become very powerful magical substances when used in spells — you will never look at chilli powder, cardamom or black pepper in the same way again!

Among the list given below of common herbs and spices used in spells, can be found the less common, together with their botanical names and suggestions for where you may find them. Many fresh herbs and flowers are also used in making magical bath mixtures and charms of every description. These can be obtained in supermarkets and florists.

ALLSPICE *(Eugenia pimentia or Pimentia officinalis)* is a distinctive culinary spice often found in cakes and pastries. Allspice is also known as Pimento.

ANISEED *(Pimpinella anisum)* is often used in Indian cookery and as a herbal tea. This spice can be found in herb and spice stores as well as those selling herbal teas.

BALM *(Melissa officinalis)* is most often used as a medicinal tea and can generally be found in stores selling health foods.

BAY LEAVES *(Laurus noblis)* are also known as bay laurel leaves and laurel leaves. They are a common cooking herb used extensively in French cuisine. The dried leaves are usually found in the supermarket with other cooking herbs.

BORAGE *(Borago officinalis)* is also known as bugloss and is used fresh in cooking. It is also sold dry as a herbal tea.

CARDAMON *(Ellateria cardamomum)* is often used in Indian cooking. The dried seed pods can usually be found in supermarkets.

CATNIP *(Nepeta cataria)* is said to intoxicate cats by its smell. It is most often found in stores selling herbal teas — it can also be found in well-stocked pet stores.

CAYENNE PEPPER *(Capsicum minimum)* a hot spice made of ground chillies or hot peppers, is often used in Mexican cooking and can be found in most supermarkets.

CHAMOMILE *(Anethemis noblis)* can be found as a herbal tea in health food stores.

CHRYSANTHEMUM *(Chrysanthemum Spp.)* known primarily as a garden flower, is often overlooked as a medicinal herb. However it can often be found packaged as a herbal tea.

CLOVER *(Trifolium* Spp*.)* a common garden weed, has medicinal properties. As a dried herb, clover can often be found as a herbal tea in health food stores.

CLOVES *(Eugenia caryophyllata)* are not to be confused with garlic cloves. They are the flower buds of a tree related to that from which allspice is taken. Clove powder or whole cloves can be found in supermarkets as a spice.

DANDELION *(Taraxacum officinalis)* is a garden weed often sold as a coffee substitute in health food stores.

DILL SEEDS *(Anethum graveolens)* are pungent seeds often used in Indian cuisine. The dried seeds can be found in most supermarkets.

EYEBRIGHT *(Euphrasia officinalis)* is sold as a herbal tea in health food stores.

FENNEL SEED *(Foeniculum vulgaris)* with its distinctive licorice-like aroma, is a common cooking herb used in Indian cooking and can be found in most supermarkets.

FENUGREEK *(Trigonella foenum graecum)* is used in Indian cookery and can be found in most supermarkets.

HAWTHORN *(Crataegus* Spp.*)* berries from the hawthorn tree can be found as a herbal tea in most health food stores.

HOREHOUND *(Marubium vulgaris)* tea can often be found in health food stores.

JASMINE *(Jasminum officinalis)* is a sweetly scented flower often found growing in warmer climates. Dried jasmine can be found packaged as a herbal tea. Chinese Jasmine tea is actually ordinary black tea scented with jasmine petals and is not a suitable substitute for pure jasmine.

LAVENDER *(Lavandula officinalis)* as dried flower heads with a beautiful scent, can generally be found in stores selling art, craft and pot pouri supplies.

LEMONGRASS *(Cymbopogon citratus)* is frequently used in South East Asian cooking. The reed can often be purchased raw, dried or powdered in stores selling oriental cooking supplies as well as in large supermarkets.

LICORICE ROOT or POWDER *(Glycyrrhiza glabra)* is often sold as a herbal tea and as a dried spice for use in biscuits and pastries. Large supermarkets and health food stores may stock this item.

NETTLES *(Urtica dioica)* are used as a tea for skin complaints in herbalism and can generally be found in health food stores.

ORRISROOT POWDER *(Iris florentina)* is the powdered violet scented root of the iris flower. It is sold in most stores selling art, craft and pot pourri supplies, for it is frequently used to stabilize the fragrance of other dried herbs and spices used in pot pourri.

PATCHOULI *(Pogostemon patchouli)* is sold in most stores selling art, craft and pot pourri supplies.

RASPBERRY LEAF *(Rubus idaeus)* is used in herbalism as a tea and can be found in health food stores.

SAFFRON *(Crocus sativum)* the world's most expensive spice, is the dried flower stamens of the autumn crocus lily. Stores selling gourmet cooking supplies should stock saffron. Bastard saffron is actually safflower and is not a suitable substitute.

SARSAPARILLA *(Smilax apera)* is often used in herbalism as a tea and can be found in health food stores.

TANSY *(Tanacetum vulgaris)* is a common garden flower but can also be found as a herbal tea in health food stores.

VALERIAN *(Valeriana officinalis)* the somewhat unpleasantly scented root of a herb, is believed to promote sleep when taken as tea. It is frequently available in health food stores.

VERVAIN *(Verbena officinalis)* is a very magical plant used frequently in herbalism and can be found in health food stores. It is also known as verbena and holy herb.

Intuition

Intuition is an essential part of spellcrafting. We all have the ability to hear from our higher selves how to make the right decisions, but first we must learn to still our minds. When we still our minds to its continual chatter, we can hear the softer tone of our inner voice — the voice of our higher selves, that part of us that is connected to the rest of humanity and to the universe itself.

Meditation techniques of one sort or another are used by magicians all over the world for this purpose. One of the easiest methods is to sit quietly in a comfortable chair by the light of a candle. Close the eyes and take three deep breaths in through the nose and out through the mouth.

Silently repeat the following:

"I dedicate this moment to the powers of pure white light and allow the stream of universal energy to course through me unhindered by trivial and harmful thoughts.
This quiet moment connects me to the core of creative energy."

Take ten deep breaths counting from ten to one. When you are ready, open your eyes and begin your day or use this peaceful moment to begin a spell.

When repeated daily this method has marvelous effects. It can open our eyes to the beauty that exists everywhere, so often unnoticed. It can help make us feel and even look more youthful. Most importantly it allows the truth of the higher self to be unveiled.

This method will also open the psychic points on your body.

Learn to trust your insights and in time you will find that the voice of your intuition will be clear and unmistakable.

Visualization

Another essential technique of spellcrafting is visualization. Spells may be regarded as keys to unlocking powerful energy that through the manipulation of symbols may be directed towards a desired result. The ability to feel magic working and to direct it by visualizing the outcome exactly as you would like weaves more potent magic than using precisely the right ingredients.

A successful spell is like a journey: the ingredients and actions are the vehicle, intuition is the map, visualization is the fuel and the outcome is the arrival.

In visualizing the outcome of a spell in fine detail and experiencing the joy of success before the outcome has happened, you are letting the universe know what you would like in your life. The universe is often very accommodating of your goals when you know what is best for yourself. At the end of every spell, and for as long as it takes afterward, imagine the outcome as you would like it in as much detail as possible.

Fear of failure and pessimism are forms of visualizing an outcome which all too often attracts misfortune. Make a pact with yourself that at least for the period in which you perform your spell and for three weeks afterward you will suspend disbelief, substitute negativity with positive thoughts, and look forward to achieving your goal. Recognize that if your spell is not successful the universe has decided in its wisdom that your goal is not beneficial to you and that something far better is in store.

Visualization is very simple, for if you can dream and imagine, you can visualize. The basic difference is that when visualizing you must fully believe you can achieve the goal at hand, then empower it with continuing positive thoughts. To this you can add the potency of spells for an even more powerful outcome.

Love

It is the contention of most mediums, spiritualists and psychics of every variety that our purpose as souls incarnated on earth is to discover the true meaning of love. It has even been said there are but two motivating forces in the human psyche — love and fear — and that every human action is the result of one or the other. If we were to go through all the ancient and modern manuscripts dealing with spells and magic it is likely that the overwhelming number of spells and rituals would be concerned with winning the love of another or keeping love alive within a relationship.

Perhaps the reason why so many people do not have their fill of love is because they are caught up in a web of its opposite — fear. Fear can make us jealous, resentful, afraid to show another how we feel in case of rejection, afraid even to love.

Before practicing any of the spells on the following pages I strongly recommend you ask yourself some hard questions. Do you wish to win the love of another because you think you are supposed to be in love? Do you think that being loved is going to give you identity?

If you want to enjoy all that love has to offer, begin by saying the following affirmation at least twenty times a day for one week:

"I am a magnet for love, love is within me, without me, before me and behind me. I AM LOVE."

At the end of the week you will find that you feel stronger and more confident of your ability to attract love. This is the time to get ready to experience the greatest gift the universe can give a human being.

A Love Powder

Love powder can be clandestinely sprinkled on the belongings of a desired person and then in your own underwear drawer to forge a psychic love bond between you. This particular recipe is from the Caribbean and involves a number of herbs and oils.

To a handful of talcum powder add the following:

- *five drops of rose oil*
- *five drops of sandalwood oil*
- *seven drops of lavender oil*
- *a teaspoon of powdered cardamom seed*
- *a teaspoon of powdered allspice*
- *a teaspoon of crushed and dried lavender*
- *a teaspoon of crushed and dried rose petals*

Mix all the ingredients together in a ceramic bowl with a fork. As you mix, visualize warm pink light building and radiating out from the powder. Gently pour the powder into a little jar and take it with you to sprinkle a little on the belongings of the person you desire. Be sure to sprinkle a pinch of the powder on yourself every day after bathing.

This powder may also be used in a little charm to keep a friend or lover thinking about you while he or she is absent.

Place a small mound of the powder on the palm of your hand while standing within a sunny spot in a natural setting. Blow a little of the powder towards each of the four cardinal points (north, south, east, west), willing the beloved to feel the pull of your love and soon return.

The most effective magical charms, powders and oils intended for use in love spells are said to be created on a Friday, the sacred day of the planet Venus, the astrological patron of love.

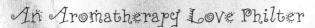

An Aromatherapy Love Philter

The following heady blend of luscious essential oils is best burned in an aromatherapy oil burner in a room where lovers are to meet. The blend is believed to be pleasing to the spirits of love and may inspire lovers to enhance their lovemaking. The recipe is based on a Caribbean love oil worn by young girls wishing to enchant their lovers.

To an oil burner full of water add the following:

✡ *two drops of essential oil of patchouli*
✡ *two drops of essential oil of orange*
✡ *two drops of essential oil of cinnamon*
✡ *a hint of essential oil of clove*

If you wish to wear this blend of essential oils on your skin as a love perfume, add the specified number of drops of each to three teaspoons (15 ml) of pure virgin olive oil and shake well.

This love formula may be modified slightly and turned into a very potent attraction oil with the addition of two drops of essential oil of vetiver. The modified formula can be anointed on thirteen small red candles to draw a person near and fill them with longing. The name of the desired person is recited one hundred and sixty nine times over the candles. With each recitation the magic should grow stronger and actually become palpable. When the energy has reached its peak by the final recitation blow the candles out to ground the magic.

A curious little charm from Mexico said to attract a lover uses a dried hummingbird wrapped in a red cloth. The charm is carried on one's person and is said to make desirous males or females buzz around the bearer.

A Charm to Bring Back a Stray Lover

The southern American state of Louisiana conjures up images of stately mansions surrounded by ancient trees fringed with Spanish moss. It is also in Louisiana that powerful magic has been woven for centuries. The warm, moist climate of the deep south of America is believed to be highly conducive to magical vibrations. Spells cast and created there are held by some psychics and magicians to be among the most potent on earth. The spiritual heartland of Southern-style magic is Africa, and the spells of the South often have a distinctly African flavor.

The following spell is remarkably simple and employs only a few basic ingredients in addition to a good deal of creative visualization.

In Louisiana it is believed that five red candles burned before the photograph of a missing loved one will draw him or her back to you.

Arrange the candles in a circle and smear each with honey, and dust them with sugar and cinnamon powder.

Light the candles and carefully place the photograph in the middle of the circle. Call the name of the truant lover exactly one hundred and nine times as the candles burn and visualize him or her returning to you with both an open heart and open arms.

Allow the candles to burn away to nothing at which time the photograph should be wrapped in a red cloth and placed beneath the bed.

Another similar method involves piercing a photograph with exactly thirty brand new fishing hooks and placing it in a jar of honey mixed with perfume. The whole jar may then be placed within a circle of five red candles.

A Spell to Keep a Lover or Spouse Faithful

The following spell is a typical prescription given to an unhappy young man or woman in Dixie roughly one hundred years ago by a spiritualist. The spell has been handed down by word of mouth to the present day and is characteristic of spells from America's South designed to keep a lover or spouse faithful.

Each ingredient has an obvious symbolic function: the rose water and sugar are intended to keep the straying lover "sweet" on the one left behind, while the ginger powder is believed to rekindle passion in the relationship. The cinnamon and cardamom powders are traditionally used in love magic to inspire thoughts of faithfulness and love. Lastly, the yellow ribbon is a token of "forget-me-not" and is used to "tie" the straying lover to your side with thoughts of love.

Take a few of his or her hairs from a recently used hair brush. Place the hairs in a bottle or jar filled with the following:

- ✡ *rose water*
- ✡ *seventeen teaspoons of sugar*
- ✡ *a teaspoon of ground ginger root*
- ✡ *a teaspoon of ground cinnamon*
- ✡ *a teaspoon of powdered cardamom seed*

With all ingredients inside, place the lid on the bottle.

Rub the bottle or jar with a sweet smelling oil and tie a yellow ribbon around it. Place the bottle under the bed shared by the couple.

A Bewitchment to Revive a Lusterless Relationship

The following spell makes use of crystals rather than herbs. Like the previous spell you will need some of your lover's hairs taken from a hair brush, a 4 inch (10 cm) square of red cotton or flannel and a needle and red thread. You will also need a small piece each of the following crystals:

✡ *aventurine*
✡ *rose quartz*
✡ *citrine*

If for any reason you cannot obtain aventurine use gold iron pyrites or fool's gold.

Take the hairs obtained from the hair brush and tie them to a few of your own, so that you have a small lock of hair knotted in the center. Place the hairs and crystals in the center of the cotton or flannel and, if you like, add a few love herbs such as rose petals, orange blossoms, jasmine flowers or any sweetly scented bloom.

Sew the contents of your charm into a small bag so that the edges are completely sealed. Hold the bag in your hands and blow on it three times. Anoint the bag with a fragrant oil or perfume and envision it suffused in a glorious pink light.

Place the charm bag underneath the bed, now and then taking it out to reanoint it with your chosen perfume or essence.

A little rose water and honey added to the final rinse of a lover's clothes in the wash promotes loving thoughts when the clothes are worn.
Freshly picked rose petals added to a bath full of water to be shared by a couple are a traditional aphrodisiac said to incite love and affection.

A Charm to Discourage the Unwanted Attentions of Another

There are times when all of us may be found to be highly appealing to another while we are already happily involved in a loving relationship. Such attention may be both unwanted and possibly even destructive to the present relationship.

The following spell is characteristic of the "sympathetic magic" of New Orleans and is said to discourage unwanted advances most effectively.

It requires a few herbs which will be used to make a "go away" powder, a red candle, three sugar cubes and a photograph of the person whose advances you wish to discourage.

This spell will not harm the person in any way.

Take the photograph and smear it with butter or oil, wrap it in a dark-colored cloth and set it aside.

Add the following ingredients to a saucepan:

✡ *a teaspoon of chilli powder*
✡ *a teaspoon of black pepper*
✡ *a teaspoon of paprika powder*
✡ *a teaspoon of cayenne pepper*

Dry roast the spices together for a brief moment over a very hot stove, being careful not to burn them. When the spices have cooled, place the mixture in a jar.

Position the photograph on the floor, remove its dark shroud and place a small red candle next to it. Using the "go away" powder, draw a circle around the photograph, light the candle and whisper the following thirteen times:

"Go from me hence and find thee another."

Leave the charm in place until the candle has burned out, take the photograph to running water (a stream or canal) and toss it in closely followed by three sugar cubes.

Prosperity

Prosperous thoughts generate prosperity. It is a dangerous thing to focus on what is lacking in our lives for this only brings more of the same. We are moved in the direction of our central thoughts, for these are what the universe uses to decide what we want in our lives. To be given the gift of affluence by the universe you must be firm in your conviction to ask for wealth and joy in your words, deeds and thoughts.

Many people who have tried methods of positive thinking have been thoroughly unsuccessful. The reason for this is that their words, thoughts and deeds have been affirming different things. There is no use in reciting positive affirmations about being wealthy and successful while at the same time penny-pinching, for this tells the universe that what you say and what you believe are very different matters. This results in a confused mixture of bounty and lack.

And this is the state in which many people who attempt positive thinking and visualization exercises find themselves. Money may come into their lives in larger than normal amounts but goes out again just as quickly.

In order to house the energy of prosperity there must be no evidence of words or deeds based in fear, motivated by thoughts of lack and want. For this reason it is crucial to be highly specific in your direction.

When you need a certain amount of money to accomplish a particular aim, a spell may be used to acquire the wealth required. It is in this achievement of a person's objectives, dreams and goals that prosperity may be found.

Prosperity Oil

Prosperity formulas usually make use of herbs thought to be under the influence of Jupiter, the planet of bounty and abundance.

This classic prosperity oil has been used for at least one hundred years by the "Hoodoo's" or followers of the magical tradition of New Orleans. The oil is traditionally compounded on a Thursday, the sacred day of the planet Jupiter, and is believed to be most effective if allowed to sit for three weeks after being mixed in a cool dark place.

Bank and cheque books, contracts, letters and share certificates may be anointed with a tiny drop of the oil to draw wealth. A small piece of green cloth anointed with the oil may be stored in the purse or wallet.

The oil may be worn as a perfume or, with the omission of the base oil, added to an aromatherapy oil burner.

Please ensure you use as little cinnamon oil as possible if the perfume is made with the intention to be worn on the skin, as cinnamon essential oil may burn.

To a dark glass bottle add the following:

✿ *one part basil powder*
✿ *one part spearmint essential oil*
✿ *one quarter part cinnamon essence*
✿ *six parts base oil (virgin olive, sunflower or light mineral)*

Mix all ingredients carefully and decant into a glass bottle. Allow the mixture to sit for at least three weeks after which it may be strained through cheesecloth or muslin to remove the basil powder residue.

Keep a small coin in the oil bottle or jar and ensure you store the oil away from the rays of the sun.

> *A sprig of basil, a magnet and five small coins placed above the threshold are said to invite the energies of prosperity into the home.*

Water of Plenty

Magical waters are extensively used in the magical traditions of the Caribbean and the United States where they are procured through mail order and retail outlets servicing the needs of the magically-minded.

Waters are given exotic names and are intended for use in the bath, wash and scrub water.

A quarter cup of Water of Plenty may be added to the bath, wash and scrub water to draw the energies of prosperity to the home, self and all members of the household.

On a Thursday evening prepare the following ingredients:

- *a handful of cinnamon powder*
- *a small handful of allspice or pimento powder*
- *a handful of dried basil leaves*
- *a handful of dried mint leaves*
- *an entire orange rind*
- *sugar*
- *a teaspoon of green food dye*
- *a cup of alcohol (ordinary household alcohol such as methylated spirit may be used)*

Add all ingredients, minus the alcohol and food dye, to a large saucepan filled with water. Boil the mixture together for half an hour, adding more liquid when needed. Set the saucepan aside to cool after boiling.

Decant the strained mixture into a bottle with a lid and add ten coins of small denomination, the alcohol and food dye. Shake well before each use.

Jars or bottles of magical waters are a wonderful place in which to keep crystals. The crystals impart their energies into the water and the water purifies and strengthens the powers of the crystals. Prosperity crystals which may be stored in a jar of Water of Plenty include amethyst, sapphire, turquoise and lodestone. Remove the crystals from the water every now and then and carry them about with you when in need of a little extra wealth.

Jovial Talisman of Wealth and Abundance

In the ancient world magicians often forged potent spells using talismans which are specially created magical devices said to attract a particular influence into the life of the bearer. A talisman is different from an amulet in that a talisman is designed to both represent and attract something while an amulet is created and used to repel some threat, for example the evil eye for which blue beads and eye-shaped pieces of jewellery are often used.

Talismans are often pictorial symbols or words inscribed on squares or disks of valuable metal, each having a particular assigned day for manufacture, metal, color and method of production according to the appropriate planetary influence.

Talismans for wealth are best produced on Thursdays, the sacred day of the astrological planet Jupiter, whose color is purple and whose metal is tin.

If you do not wish to go to the expense or trouble of cutting a small square of tin and painstakingly inscribing symbols (in this case numbers) into its surface then a simple yet no less powerful alternative is to use purple card and gold or silver ink.

The design is taken from an old book of magic and uses the power of numerology to draw the abundant energies of the planet Jupiter.

414151
97612
511108
162313

The talisman is to be drawn on a square of purple card small enough to fit into a purse or pocket and is to be rendered in silver or gold ink on a Thursday.

On the back of the square the image of a horseshoe and a hammer are to be drawn together with the initials of the maker.

Once drawn, the talisman is to be held in the hand by the light of a single purple candle. Pine, bergamot, cedar or sage incense should be burned and the talisman passed repeatedly through the smoke to both bless and cleanse it.

As the incense and candle burn one should visualize a stream of gold, coins and treasure falling onto the talisman which readily absorbs and stores this bounty.

If at all possible it is wise to take the consecrated talisman to the local bank and hide it where it will not be found for one night, perhaps under a doormat or in a garden. When the talisman is retrieved the next day it will have absorbed the monetary energies of the bank.

Carry the talisman in a little purple cloth or paper pouch and occasionally repeat the visualization exercise by the light of a purple candle, the air scented with incense.

A Money Magnet

Magnets are frequently used in the magic of prosperity as they are said to draw the energies of abundance on a spiritual level just as they attract metal objects on a physical level.

Many charms are rendered more effective if regularly anointed with an appropriate magical essence. The following Mexican mojo bag may be anointed with the Prosperity Oil formula previously described or may be effectively treated with essential oil of peppermint or basil.

Take a small bright green rectangle of cloth and place the following in a little mound on one side:

✡ *a sprinkling of dried basil*
✡ *a portion of golden glitter or tinsel powder*
✡ *a dash of powdered cinnamon*
✡ *a touch of dried peppermint*
✡ *a small magnet*
✡ *a teaspoon of iron filings (Iron filings may be made by filing a piece of iron over some paper to catch the falling dust).*

Fold one side of the cloth over the other to encase the herbs, magnet and iron filings. Carefully bind the edges of the cloth with a green or golden thread, being sure to fully bind the contents within.

For each stitch, chant the name of the angel of wealth "Parasiel".

Hold the bag in your hands and, with closed eyes, visualize golden light emanating from it, growing stronger and radiating out to fill the room.

Light a green candle and recite the following prayer to Parasiel with the charm in hand:

"Sweet and Glorious angel Parasiel be ye before me and aft, to the left of me and to the right. Bless and cleanse this charm made in your honor and let it be for me a magnet for wealth and abundance. By your name, so be it."

Carry the charm on your person from then on. Anoint the charm every Thursday with Prosperity Oil, reciting the prayer to Parasiel each time.

Traditional Prosperity Charms and Omens

There are many little folk spells and omens concerning prosperity some of which make good magical sense and others which are merely quaint curiosities.

Below can be found a sample of some of the many folk customs associated with prosperity and wealth.

- ✿ Should a cricket stray into the home, do not disturb or remove it as it foretells great wealth and success. Welcome the cricket with a fond greeting and let it travel about the home of its own accord.
- ✿ At the stroke of midnight on New Year's Eve stand outside the front door with a handful of coins and toss them through the threshold into the house to bring wealth and joy for the coming year.
- ✿ Sprinkle peppermint tea about the home to attract the gnomes, the little earth spirits whose gift is wealth and health.
- ✿ An occasional dab of essential oil of bergamot on bank books is said to keep the finances healthy.
- ✿ A tiny red spider if found crawling on the hand betokens great wealth from a creative endeavor, for this is the fabled money spider.
- ✿ If one has accidentally put an article of clothing on the wrong way around, wealth and success are sure to follow.
- ✿ A buckeye or horse chestnut, which is also known as a conker, is a very potent prosperity charm. Carry one on your person at all times but be sure to never eat the horse chestnut as it is toxic.
- ✿ A ginseng root shaped like a little human is a talisman of wealth, especially when carried in a purple mojo or charm bag with a magnet and a coin.
- ✿ Sleep with some fresh spearmint beneath the bed to dream up schemes for wealth and luxury.
- ✿ Wear an article of purple clothing, perhaps a tie or handkerchief, to business meetings where financial matters are to be discussed, as this attracts the abundant blessings of the planet Jupiter.
- ✿ Bathe in water to which a handful of coins has been added to cloak the self in the energies of prosperity.

Luck and Success

The magic of luck refers to charms and spells associated with gambling and there are literally thousands upon thousands of recorded rites, charms and rituals intended to sway chance in the direction of a specific person's favor.

When we say luck is on our side we are admitting that a successful outcome may owe more to chance than anything else. Magically speaking we can facilitate chance through spells and the action of charms to lead us into situations that may prove valuable in the course of our goals.

To be successful we must have a goal to reach, for success can only be found in the expected and worked for achievement. Success inevitably eludes us when we are not driven towards a goal. Success is a journey and requires a destination.

Visualizing the self as successful in whatever terms "successful" means for you is crucial in spellcraft. It is not enough to simply dream of achieving a goal.

In order for the dream to be a visualization (and therefore a potent aid in the quest) the starting point must be a firm belief that the goal can be achieved. This belief may be brought about by looking at the desired end in all facets imaginable and knowing that its achievement is not impossible and requires only a set of basic steps forward. Where spellcraft may help in this process is in the details. If it is crucial for your goals to meet the right people or to be in the right situation the spells that follow may be of great aid.

Spells and charms designed to maximize our inbuilt drive towards success can be found in the pages that follow as can those designed to sway the fickle nature of chance in gambling matters.

Formulas for Luck and Success

Recipes for luck and success very often contain citrus based essences as these are said to court the favor of the mercurial energies of chance. In the following two formulas, both of which are typical of commercial products sold in magical supply houses, the citrus flavor comes from citronella which is often used in aromatherapy as an insect repellent. If this particular essence is not available to you, you may like to substitute it with essential oil of lemongrass.

Fortuna Oil

To a glass bottle add the following:

✿ *one part frankincense absolute oil*
✿ *one part lemon essential oil*
✿ *two parts lavender essence*
✿ *one eighth part citronella essential oil*
✿ *a few whole aniseeds or saffron threads to the bottle*
✿ *eight parts light mineral oil as a base*

Fortuna oil is especially good for anointing lucky charms, talismans, rabbit's feet, yellow and orange lucky candles. It is also said to dispose the energies of luck in your favor when rubbed on the palms of the hands before playing games of chance.

A typical Puerto Rican practice is to buy a lottery ticket and place it beneath a candlestick holding a dripless yellow candle anointed with this oil. The candle should be held in the hand and anointed from the middle of the shaft to the top and then from the middle to the base, as this symbolically addresses the wish for luck to heaven and then to the energies of manifestation on earth.

Cornucopia Powder

This powder should be sprinkled over the head and about the home when a change of fortune is needed. When carried in a little yellow paper envelope to meetings and interviews it is said to draw the energies of success to the bearer.

It is also used in a special success charm made with an apple.

To a glass jar add the following:

✡ *one part basil powder*
✡ *one part spearmint powder*
✡ *one part aniseed powder*
✡ *one half part nutmeg powder*
✡ *five parts talcum powder*
✡ *one eighth part citronella essential oil*

Write a brief description of your goal or aim on a tiny piece of paper and roll the paper into a miniature scroll.

Using an apple corer, bore a hole halfway into an apple and retain the piece of apple removed. Insert the scroll into the hole together with a sprinkling of Cornucopia Powder and replace the apple "plug" removed when drilling the hole into the apple.

Place the apple in a jar and cover it completely with white sugar and white wine. Place the lid on the jar and pray for success.

Put the jar beneath the bed or within a bedside cabinet. As the apple, sugar and wine ferments, so too does the energy of your goal.

Four Winds Wishing Spell

There are many spells designed to carry a secret wish into the universe where the productive powers of creation can bring its realization into being. Nearly all such spells make use of the tremendously powerful process of creative visualization.

The following spell courts the favor of the four winds or the energies of the compass points. For this spell you will need to ascertain North and from there you can easily find South (if facing North, South is behind you). Also when facing North you can readily locate East and West, East being to your right and West to your left.

The four winds were given magical names by the ancient Greeks — Boreas, Eureus, Notus and Zephyrus — it is these forces together with those of the elemental spirits of air, water, fire and earth, that are called upon in the spell to carry your wish to the four points of the universe.

The spell is designed to be performed outside and you will require any one of the following powdered herbs:

✡ *bay, also known as bay laurel (for success and prestige wishes)*
✡ *rosemary (for promotion and advancement wishes)*
✡ *cinnamon (for power wishes)*
✡ *vervain (verbena) (for general wishes)*
✡ *cardamom (for love wishes)*
✡ *peppermint (for prosperity wishes)*

Having chosen the appropriate herb hold it in your hands and visualize the achievement of your goal in fine detail. Hold the herb to your mouth and breathe upon it trying to force the wish through your breath into the very structure of the herb.

When you are satisfied turn to the North and say:

"King Boreas of the North Wind, by the powers of earth,
I call you to carry my wish to the Northern quarter,
and by the powers of the gnomes, I ask that you bring me success."

Blow a quarter of the powdered herb from your palm
in the direction of North.

Turn to the East and say:

"King Eureus of the East Wind, by the powers of air,
I call you to carry my wish to the Eastern quarter,
and by the powers of the sylphs, I ask that you bring me success."

Blow a quarter of the powdered herb from your
palm in the direction of East.

Turn to the South and say:

"King Notus of the South Wind, by the powers of fire, I call you to carry my
wish to the Southern quarter, and by the powers of the salamanders, I ask
that you bring me success."

Blow a quarter of the powdered herb in the direction of South.

Turn to the West and say:

"King Zephyrus of the West Wind, by the powers of water, I call you to carry
my wish to the Western quarter, and by the powers of the undines, I ask that
you bring me success."

Blow the final quarter of herb from your palm in the direction of West.

The spell is ended. Leave the area without looking back, safe in the
knowledge that the powers of the universe have taken over your wish.

A Key to Respect and Favor

Pieces of enchanted jewelry, symbolically empowered to draw desirable conditions into the life of the bearer, have a place in virtually every magical and religious tradition known to humanity.

The following talisman is made with an old fashioned key worn about the neck on a chain or cord. Such keys may be obtained in junk or antique stores and are generally inexpensive. Find a key that pleases you but make sure that it is small enough to be worn about the neck.

Once you have found your key, bathe it in a strong salt and water mixture to remove any psychic impurities and bury it in the earth overnight to align its energies to the productive powers of the earth.

Retrieve the key and wash it well. Next you will be required to take a walk around your neighbourhood with key in hand. The key must touch the door or gate of a number of locations believed to hold immense psychic power. By touching the key to the threshold of each of these locations, it draws into itself some of the energy housed within each. As you are to wear the key, you will win the respect, authority and dignity of those around you.

The key must touch the door or gate of each of the following:

✿ *a courthouse*
✿ *a police station*
✿ *a doctor's surgery*
✿ *a bank*
✿ *a fire station*
✿ *a shop*
✿ *and lastly a graveyard*

The key is worn around the neck on a chain or cord from then on. From time to time you may like to anoint the key with Fortuna Oil to keep it fully charged with magical energy.

Traditional Gambling Charms

There are a countless number of charms, roots, crystals, herbs and formulas said to give the faithful user command over the whimsical fall of the dice or the spin of the wheel, however such charms often have the annoying habit of working for a brief time and then suddenly ceasing to work right when the biggest win is anticipated. Perhaps this occurs because there must always be a balance between both good and poor fortune. What follows is a sample of the most popular traditional gambling charms.

✧ A Hi John the Conqueror root (a Mexican species of morning glory from Xalapa) carried in a yellow charm bag and anointed with a commercial luck oil is possibly the most popular gambling charm in the modern world. These now rare roots are sold in magical supply houses all over the world.

✧ Some crystals and stones said to draw luck include gold iron pyrites (fool's gold), aventurine, magnetite, siderite (both of which are referred to as "lodestone") and citrine. The stones should be carried in the purse or wallet for luck.

✧ Lodestones which are natural magnets are very popular gambling charms and are generally carried in pairs in little yellow or gold cloth bags. One lodestone is said to draw good luck and the other to banish misfortune. The stones must be fed with iron filings or magnetic sand and the bags in which they are carried should be anointed with a lucky formula such as Fortuna Oil (see page 34).

✧ A traditional New Orleans charm consists of a nutmeg with a hole bored halfway into its surface. The hole is filled with mercury or quicksilver and is plugged with molten wax. *A word of caution: mercury (quicksilver) is highly toxic and should never come into contact with the skin, eyes or mouth. For this reason the hole in the nutmeg should be plugged with polyester resin or another synthetic filler with properties of extreme strength and durability.*

✧ A red flannel or chamois bag filled with a wishbone (from the back of a chicken), a pebble taken from a graveyard and a ginseng root is said to draw strong good fortune.

Protection

Some spellcasters believe that ignoble human motives like spite, envy and hatred are the effects of the intervention of negative energies and many spells have been created to absorb, destroy, ward off and cast them out.

The belief in the evil eye is based in southern Europe and all kinds of charms may be seen in Italy and Greece to ward off this menace. It is believed that some people are born with the ability to devastate the joy of others with nothing more than a passing glance. A person with the evil eye is said to be possessed by the spirit of envy, and even a fleeting look can sink a boat at sea, sour milk, render breeding stock infertile, and cause a crop to wither and perish.

Traditional charms against the evil eye include a tiny horn carried in the pocket, a glass eye or a single blue bead on a chain around the neck and even a hand signal where the fist is closed and the thumb is thrust between the index and middle fingers. Little figa hands are often rendered in gold or silver and worn about the neck.

Blue and white eyes are rendered in jewelry, painted on houses and boats and molded into brass charms to be hung on the bridles of horses. These charms are believed to draw the gaze of the evil eye away from the target towards the charm.

Magical powders, oils and charms can be worn or carried to protect against vampires. In magic the term "vampire" refers to an often unwitting person who drains the psychic energy from others leaving the victim depressed, worn or even sickly. Such people absorb the life force out of a room or person and use it to bolster their own energy level.

For spellcasters, magical measures of protection are a matter of course.

SATOR
AREPO
TENET
OPERA
ROTAS

Protection Oil

At times we all feel threatened by outside forces, be they physical, spiritual or nothing more than a vague feeling of danger. At such times it is wise to safeguard the self by wearing a traditional formula designed to ward off negative energies and discourage the bad intentions of shady people.

The following recipe is typical of formulas sold in magical supply houses all around the world. The formula uses essential oils aligned with the planets Mars and Saturn, which are astrologically suited to the purpose.

To a glass bottle add the following:

✡ *one part cedarwood essential oil*
✡ *one part sage or rosemary essential oil*
✡ *two parts sandalwood essence*
✡ *four white pepper corns*
✡ *six parts base oil (virgin olive, sunflower or light mineral)*

The oil may be worn on the skin or, with the omission of the base oil, added to an aromatherapy oil burner, or mixed with paraffin and used in an oil burning lamp.

For a more robust effect, dab a drop of the oil on the bark of a tall oak, silently asking the spirit of the tree for protection and courage. By way of thanks, leave four coins of small denomination by the roots.

Sage leaves hung above the threshold are said to trap dark energies and prevent them entering the home. Sage tea with salt added may be sprinkled about the home in every nook and cranny when it is perceived that evil energies have infested the place.

A Mexican Charm Bag for Protection

Mojo or charm bags are frequently employed in Mexican magic and are designed and carried for almost every purpose.

The following mojo bag is used to protect against all harm both physical and psychic. The charm is made in honor of the Mexican saint of protection Santa Marta, and its manufacture includes a special prayer said to surround the devout in a shield of protective energy.

Take a small vivid red square of cloth and fold it in half so that two corners come together on two sides. The result should be a rectangle large enough to be sewn into a small bag suitable for carrying in the purse or pocket. Place the following in a little mound on one side of the rectangle of cloth:

✡ *a pinch of white pepper*
✡ *a portion of sage*
✡ *a sprinkling of powdered garlic*
✡ *a dash of cayenne pepper*
✡ *a little morsel of tobacco*
✡ *a thorn from a cactus or rose*
✡ *a small tiger's or cat's eye stone*

Fold one side of the cloth over the other to encase the herbs and crystal inside. Carefully sew around the edges of the cloth, being careful to thoroughly bind the contents within. Kiss the charm, place it beneath your pillow and sleep on it over four consecutive nights.

Hold the charm bag in your hands and with closed eyes, visualize brilliant red energy emanating from it, growing stronger and radiating out to fill the room.

Light a red candle and recite the following prayer to Santa Marta:

"Sanctified Santa Marta, bless and cleanse me of my woes.
Slay the dragon of my misfortune and light my way upon the path
to peace and tranquillity. Bless my charm and occasion it to
protect me against all harm in your name."

Carry the charm on your person from then on.

A Talisman for Protection

Talismans like that which follow have been used by the magically-minded from time immemorial. The particular design and method of use for the talisman below is adapted from the famous "Key of Solomon the King" one of the oldest magical textbooks known to humankind. This talisman has been used by the followers of Solomon for centuries as protection from all kinds of negative forces. The design is said to be the most perfect double acrostic in existence — the words can be read on any possible horizontal or vertical plane and remain true.

A rough translation for the words would be "Sator, sower of the seed, spins the wheel" which may mean that when a human being expends some effort in the direction of a true goal, the universe will match the effort and the goal will be achieved.

The talisman must be drawn on a piece of black card small enough to fit into a purse or pocket and is to be rendered in gold ink on a Saturday after dark.

S A T O R
A R E P O
T E N E T
O P E R A
R O T A S

Once drawn, the talisman is to be held in the hand by the light of a single white candle. Frankincense incense should be burned and the talisman passed repeatedly through the smoke to bless and cleanse it.

A sincere prayer to King Solomon asking for protection against all harm should be improvised and psalm number 70 recited over the talisman.

Once consecrated, the talisman should be wrapped in a piece of black silk and carried upon your person for as long as you feel in need of protection.

Miscellaneous Protection Charms

There are countless little charms and amulets used to protect yourself and your property from harm. Some of the more effective are outlined below.

- ✿ Mistletoe, also known as golden bough, carried in a little hand sewn cloth bag is a traditional Celtic method of protecting the self and is also used by the followers of the magic from America's South.
- ✿ Marjoram or wild oregano is believed to absorb dangerous negative energies when powdered and sprinkled about the home. In Italy the followers of Italian witchcraft or stregeria make this herb into a tea and add it to the wash and scrub water to protect the home and its inhabitants.
- ✿ Cuban and Puerto Rican followers of the folk religion known as santería regularly burn brown sugar, a pinch of sulphur and garlic powder on charcoal within their homes to cleanse them of any negative energy. When the home has been cleansed it is protected by praying to Santa Barbara, the saint of protection, by the light of a red and a white candle.
- ✿ A pinch of sulphur powder and cayenne pepper carried in a little brown paper pouch upon which a sword has been drawn, can be carried to ward off hostile words and deeds.
- ✿ Plain bluing (used to whiten clothes in the wash) is said to ward off evil spirits in the magic of America's South. The bluing is generally carried in a little blue paper pouch.
- ✿ When a little sulphur and blue metal stone (the type often used in the process of making concrete) are added to bluing and carried in a blue cloth pouch, the charm is said to simultaneously ward off evil and attract lucky energies to the bearer.
- ✿ Mirrors are said to frighten away dark spirits and tiny pieces of silvered glass are often sewn into Indian cotton dresses as are bells which are also used for this purpose.
  - ✿ A tiny silver bell worn about the neck is a very potent protective charm as evil spirits cannot abide the sweet ring of any bell.
    - ✿ Travelers are especially in need of protection when in a foreign land. A tiny mirror smeared with a clove of garlic and placed beneath the bed is said to protect the sleeper when away from his or her own home. The mirror may also be carried on one's person for this same purpose.

Work

For a very large number of people in the modern world nearly half of their time and certainly a good deal more of their efforts and trials are spent working.

Often the only real connection we have with the people with whom we work and spend much of our waking hours is the work we share. Most of us have lives outside the work place which in some way or another impact on how we relate to each other on a work level.

Whenever large numbers of people are thrown together in a common cause or operation, conflicts are certain to arise. The working lives of many people are spent in angst, stemming from an inner pool of dissatisfaction with their roles as employees, managers or corporate heads.

But work should not be like this. This time should be happy, satisfying and even uplifting. Little upsets such as gossip in the office can seriously hamper harmonious and productive working lives. Unemployment or the threat of being laid off as the result of business not doing well is frightening and stressful to those in that situation and their families.

The little spells, charms and enchantments that follow cover some of the problems that may arise and can, with faithful practice, remedy them.

A Charm to Secure Employment

In this day and age one of the most soul-destroying situations that can happen to a person is also one of the most common — to be made redundant. Another is not to be given a chance to show what you are capable of in a working situation. The following charm may work wonders in securing the faithful practitioner a satisfying position, but will only do so if you are willing to go to as many interviews as you can manage.

On a Sunday take a clean handkerchief, preferably green in color, and lay it flat with one of the corners pointing toward you. Place three cardamom seeds, a bay leaf and a sprig of rosemary (or a teaspoon of the dried herb) in the center.

These herbs are believed to surround you in self-confident and attractive energy. The cardamom seeds are traditionally believed to sweeten your personality and bring out your natural eloquence. Bay leaves are the ancient Roman symbol of success and triumph while rosemary is a herb of achievement and mental alertness.

Tie the corners of the handkerchief together with a length of string so that you have a bundle of herbs small enough to carry with you to employment interviews.

Before each interview hold the little bundle and touch it to your forehead, hold it there while you close your eyes and visualize yourself walking into an interview room, radiating confidence; imagine yourself captivating the interviewers with your personality. Visualize yourself being in a position to pick and choose jobs at will.

Carry your charm in your pocket or purse to all your interviews and be sure to accept any rejections as a sign from the universe that the job was not right for you. When you come across a job that is perfect for you, your success bundle will help you get it.

A Magical Powder to Create a Harmonious Working Environment

Magical powders are a staple in the spellcaster's armory because they are easy to make and can be used surreptitiously. To make your working environment a place of harmony and creativity, the following powder should be sprinkled around when no one is looking.

Assemble the following on a Thursday evening:

✡ *three drops of rose oil*
✡ *five drops of sandalwood oil*
✡ *seven drops of lavender oil*
✡ *a handful of talcum powder*
✡ *a teaspoon of dried and powdered chamomile flowers*

Mix the oils and the chamomile together in a ceramic bowl with a fork until they are well combined. Add the talcum powder and mix well. As you mix, hum a single monotonous note and visualize warm blue light building and radiating out from the powder. Do this until you are satisfied and gently pour the powder into a little paper envelope or sachet. Take it to work the next morning.

Lime leaves hidden about a work place pacifies hostile co-workers. A sprinkling of earth under your desk helps relieve stress by grounding your energy. A dark colored crystal placed before or above a computer screen helps to absorb stress-causing vibrations emanating from the computer.

An Enchantment to Obtain a Coveted Promotion

There can be no greater reward or compliment paid to you in a working situation than to be offered a promotion with more creative control, more money and more responsibility. You may feel that you deserve a promotion for a piece of particularly good work or simply because of loyal and industrious service. The following enchantment is a traditional candle-burning spell to gain a promotion.

Purchase a yellow taper candle and a small package of sewing pins. Using one of the pins as a scribing tool, scratch the name of the position you wish to obtain lengthwise into the surface of the candle. Turn the candle over and scratch your own name into the wax with the same pin.

Smear the candle with essential oil of Bergamot and sprinkle it with golden glitter. Place the candle into a candle holder, extinguish any artificial light, light the candle and repeat the following over it:

"Forces of Light and Purity, lend unto me the capacity
to inspire, to command, to create and to understand.
Ground me in success and cloak me in victory — by the names of power —
AGLA, EL, SHADDAI, ELOHIM and TETRAGRAMMATON.
By my will so be it."

Sitting in front of the candle, close your eyes and visualize yourself in your new office, being addressed by your co-workers under the title of the position to which you aspire. Take as little or as long as you need to fully believe you have achieved your new position. Allow the candle to burn out and await with faith to accept the offer of promotion you so desire.

Remember that if you were not granted your wish, the universe has something much better in store for you.

A Spell to Deal With a Difficult Boss

Many employees are subjected to intimidatory tactics by their bosses. A high proportion of these workers feel their only recourse is to resign in the hope of finding employment in a more cordial environment. The following spell is another possible way to deal with the problem.

Obtain a piece of paper with a sample of the troublesome boss's handwriting and cut the paper into a small square. Soak the square in a mixture of ammonia and brown vinegar with a few black pepper corns added.

Allow the paper to dry thoroughly. Light a grey candle and recite the following while holding the paper in your hands:

"By the powers of universal justice you (boss's name)
may bedevil me no more. All done to me rebounds onto you and
so mote it be by the command AGLA, EL and YAHOVA."

Place the piece of paper in your shoe and ensure that you wear it to work the next day.

For a particularly difficult boss, sprinkle a pinch of the following mixture beneath his or her desk:

✡ *one part pulverised patchouli leaves*
✡ *one part powdered cayenne pepper*
✡ *one part mustard powder*
✡ *a pinch of sulphur*

It is most likely your boss's attitude towards you will greatly improve from then on. If your boss begins to become difficult again, sprinkle more of the powder beneath his or her desk.

Hostile energies directed towards you can be overcome by carrying a jet or onyx stone on your person. The stone should be washed in a salt and water mixture both before use and once a week while in use.

The Magic of Children

Children inhabit a very different world from that of adults. They exist within a universe where dynamic forces of imagination and symbolic action are much more real to them than day to day events are to most adults.

Numerous children have "imaginary" friends and many psychics believe these friends may actually be elementals, nature spirits, ghosts or even the spirits of departed loved ones.

Most spiritualists, psychics and witches believe that children are born with abilities from past lives. These abilities may take many forms and most of us can probably think of a child we know who will occasionally express something of great wisdom or who has highly developed talents that belie their young age.

Unfortunately the age of mass technology has robbed many children of the ability to make believe. Some parents even discourage fanciful notions and wild conjectures, the very stuff of the magical years of childhood. A child robbed of his or her ability to dream and imagine cannot be expected to grow into a creative and dynamic adult.

A sensitive parent can instill the most important lessons of social and moral behavior in their children while actually promoting their creativity and imagination. A child with the ability to create and imagine can become an adult capable of almost anything at all.

What follows are a number of methods for bringing out inborn abilities, encouraging the child to be all that they can and instilling a high level of self love. A child with self love is a child who will succeed and grow into an adult with a love for all humanity.

A Rite to Place a Newborn under the Guidance and Protection of the Universe

The following rite is a beautiful method of protecting a newborn baby as well as calling the universal energies of love and guidance to lead her or him through the trials of life with strength and a resolution to succeed.

On a Wednesday morning sit comfortably on the floor with the baby. Place a sweet smelling bunch of flowers beside her or him. Do not burn incense as this may alarm or irritate the child.

Close your eyes and visualize a stream of brilliant white light enshrouding you and the child. Take the child's hands in yours and recite the following:

"Forces of pure white light, spirits of the earth, of fire and water and air, be here with us and witness my pledge.
I (your name) dedicate this young life to the forces of purity, love and truth.
With peace and love I give over my child to the path of bliss and learning."

Take a flower from the bunch, hold it above the child and say:

"Forces of love please place my child under your guidance and protection, may her/his path in this life be smooth and may all his/her lessons be learned with grace and strength."

Kiss the child and enjoy the moment.

Hang the bunch of flowers to dry out. When they are dry wrap them in a white cloth and store them in a safe place.

As the child grows over the years, sprinkle a few crushed petals from the bunch of dried flowers beneath his or her bed on each birthday to call the forces of love to his or her side.

A Spell to Call a Child's Guardian Angel

The following spell is designed to invite a beloved child's guardian angel to provide a shield of protection through which the taunts and cruelty of a bully cannot penetrate. On a Sunday evening explain to the child what you are about to do together.

Gather together the following items:

✡ *a white candle*
✡ *a glass of water*
✡ *a white feather*
✡ *a white moonstone or milky quartz*

With the child's help arrange the items neatly on a table or bench. Light the candle and extinguish any artificial illumination. Close your eyes and recite the following:

"Great and pure loving spirit of guidance and protection,
angel assigned to this my child (child's name) please be here as a
beacon of strength and mighty vigilance. Let no threat or malice harm
(child's name) and shield him/her with your wings."

Place the moonstone or white crystal in the water and dip the feather into the liquid. Using the feather sprinkle some of the water over the child's head and say:

"With this sacred water of love and power I protect you
in the name of your guardian angel who looks over you
and protects you with mighty wings."

Blow out the candle and have the child carry the crystal or moonstone at all times. If the stone is lost it has served its purpose and the indication is to perform the spell once more using the same candle and feather as before. The candle and feather should be put away safely for use again if needed.

When the threat has passed, burn the candle away to nothing and thank the child's angel with an improvised prayer or chant.

A Spell to Halt Nightmares

To awaken in a state of high anxiety after a nightmare is a terrible ordeal even for most adults, but when children suffer continual nightmares the effects can be long lasting and may eventually lead to sleep disturbances.

Children are much more sensitive to psychic influences than the average adult, and nightmares, when suffered for a long period of time, may be a symptom of psychic attack. Regardless of the causes behind a child's suffering continual nightmares there is a magical solution that may prove effective. You will need:

- ✡ *a sheet of purple card or paper*
- ✡ *a black marker pen*
- ✡ *salt, water and perfume*
- ✡ *a raw potato*

Copy the following magical name on the sheet of card or paper being careful to maintain the triangular shape.

```
A B R A C A D A B R A
A B R A C A D A B R
A B R A C A D A B
A B R A C A D A
A B R A C A D
A B R A C A
A B R A C
A B R A
A B R
A B
A
```

Place the design above the child's bed being sure to explain what its intention is. Spray or sprinkle the room at least once a week with a mixture of salt, water and perfume. Each time you sprinkle the room with the mixture, if possible have the child help you recite the following:

"Guidance and love of the universe, please protect my
child (child's name) from the night terrors that assault her/him.
In your loving arms I commit my child to your protection when
he/she is asleep. I do this in the name of love and faith."

Rub any mirrors in the room with a little garlic and place an uncooked potato upon a dish beneath the child's bed. Replace the potato each week and discard it by burial. The earth in which the potato is buried will nullify the negativity which the potato has absorbed.

A Spell for Popularity

There are times in every life when finding and keeping friends is difficult and seemingly impossible. For many children this can make going to school a painful experience. Often the most gifted children are the loneliest simply because they are different. The following spell is designed to help a child become popular or at least find one or two good friends. The spell involves creating a charm to be carried upon the child's person. The charm may be made by the child or by a parent and given to the child to carry.

On a Sunday morning, take a small bright yellow rectangle of cloth and place the following in a little mound towards one side:

✡ *petals of a sunflower, marigold or other yellow flower*
✡ *a pinch of powdered vervain or spearmint*
✡ *a little powdered patchouli or a few drops of patchouli oil*
✡ *a small magnet or a magnetic lodestone*
✡ *and a teaspoon of iron filings (Iron filings may be simply made by filing a piece of iron over a piece of paper to catch the falling dust)*

A special talisman for attracting friends is also to go into the charm bag. This talisman is made by drawing the design below in gold ink on a piece of yellow card small enough to fit into the bag.

Once drawn, hold the talisman is your hand by the light of a yellow candle. Frankincense incense should be burned and the talisman passed repeatedly through the smoke to bless and cleanse it. Place the talisman on top of the pile of herbs and fold one side of the cloth over the other so as to encase the herbs, magnet and talisman inside.

Carefully bind the edges of the cloth with red thread, being sure to fully bind the contents within.

Once made the charm must be passed repeatedly through the incense smoke to empower it.

With the charm in hand, recite the following spell:

"Spirits of the glorious Sun, lend unto me thy strength of purpose and thy brilliant rays of warmth and joy. Let me be a beacon of friendliness and let me touch those whom I am in contact with the joy of connection."

Have the child carry the charm from then on anointing it from time to time with perfume or aftershave lotion. The child should never show the charm to another person as this will destroy its power.

The Home

The home should be a refuge from the trials and hectic pace of the outside world but all too often it is beleaguered by petty squabbles and rivalries.

The energy in the home may be so tense that there is little possibility of it being a soothing place in which to cast off the cares of the outside world. When this is the case it is likely that the home is suffering under the weight of a concentrated form of negative energy and the residents can do little other than react to this hostile force by being in turn hostile with each other.

Fortunately there are many magical remedies for this problem and the results can be quite amazing.

The home can be transformed into a calming and restful place of healing. Spells outlined in the following section include those for inviting the spirits of the home to help in daily matters, to bring peace and harmony to the home, to deal with difficult neighbors, to protect the home from thieves and intruders, to cleanse and purify a dwelling, growing an enchanted crop of vegetables and special aromatherapy blends for use in the home.

Mary Jones
8 Lavender Lane
Lilly pilly

A Spell To Purify and Bless a Dwelling

When taking possession of a new home it is wise to cleanse the premises of residual energy left over from previous tenants. The rite described below is a traditional European method of exorcizing this energy — it may also be used in an office or store, or in a home already occupied.

You will need a few basic materials for the rite:

✡ *incense, either stick, cone or charcoal burning*
✡ *water with added salt in a glass or dish*
✡ *bread that is regularly consumed by the self or family*
✡ *a white candle in a candle holder*
✡ *a bell, preferably with a sweet ring*

Arrange each item in a circle around you in that part of the house you consider to be the psychic hub of the dwelling — perhaps the kitchen or family room. While sitting comfortably within the middle of the circle, light the candle and incense.

Relax, breathing deeply for a moment to ground yourself, then take the salt and water mixture into your hands and say:

> *"With this salt of the earth and water of the rains I purify this place of all but the most pure and beneficent energies."*

Walk about the entire dwelling sprinkling the mixture as you go. Return to the circle and replace the salt and water. Take up the candle and say:

"With this light I bring truth and wisdom to this place."

Walk about the home with the candle and return to the circle. Take up the bell and say:

"With this bell I call forth love and joy, within this place
all are bright and happy."

Ring the bell as you move about the home. With the bread in hand say:

"In this place there is abundance and prosperity."

Leave small chunks of bread in every room. With the incense in hand say:

"With this sweet perfume I bring peace and harmony here, all words and
deeds in this place are sweet and harmonious."

Walk about the home wafting smoke into every corner.

Return to the circle and relax. Feel the energies moving and circulating within the home. Enjoy the atmosphere and when you are ready blow out the candle and put away all items used in the rite. Leave the chunks of bread strewn about the home overnight and remove them in the morning.

Mirrors should be kept
clean and well dusted as
they can become a gateway
for dark energies to enter
into the home. A smear of
garlic on the frame or glass
itself once a month will
guard against this.

A Magical Water to Bring Peace to a Troubled Home

When the home is beset by constant levels of conflict among family members it is likely that hostile energy has suffused the home. Fortunately there is a simple and inexpensive remedy for this problem which makes use of the cooling energies of a number of different enchanted waters.

Add the following to a large glass bottle with a close fitting lid:

✡ *two parts rose water*
✡ *one part sea water*
✡ *one part rain water*
✡ *one part spring water*
✡ *three parts of alcohol*
✡ *a tiny mirror or piece of mirrored glass*

The alcohol may be cane, wood spirit or methylated and is essential as it prevents the mixture turning sour. Alternatives to rose water are any one of the essences of lily of the valley, lavender, gardenia or geranium.

The mixture should be gently stirred, keeping in mind the mirror in the bottle. The following chant is then said over the mixture, preferably by the light of a blue candle:

"Powers of the sea, powers of the rain, powers of stream and field be ye to the right of me and to the left of me. Be ye before and aft and all about. Flood thy peace into this liquid of the art and bring harmony, blessed concord and tranquillity to my home. So mote it be."

At this point you may like to add a single fresh white rose to the bottle.

Walk about the home with a small dish of the water, sprinkling a little about in each room. Pour a little into a saucer and place it beneath the beds of particularly restless family members to calm and pacify.

A Spell to Compel a Troublesome Neighbor to Retreat

Well before it reaches the courts, trouble with neighbors can be dealt with by magical means. The following spell is a magical warning that if the trouble continues consequences will arise. The spell makes use of a very hot powder used to sprinkle over the threshold or front path of the neighbours home.

Add a teaspoon of each of the following ingredients to a mixing bowl:

✡ *sulphur powder*
✡ *black pepper*
✡ *ground coffee*
✡ *cayenne pepper*
✡ *garlic powder*
✡ *mustard powder (or ground mustard seed)*
✡ *a charred and powdered black feather is optional*

Mix the ingredients well while recalling the times you have felt anger towards the neighbors. Force the anger to surge up then leave, flowing through your hands into the powder. Pour the enchanted powder into a small glass jar and close the lid.

While unobserved, in the deepest darkness of night, sprinkle some of the powder over the threshold or front path of the neighbor's home. Turn and leave without looking back. Once inside your own home, turn every mirror in the house toward the wall to send back all negative energy emanating from the hostile neighbor's home.

If the trouble continues, take a pinch of dirt or dust from the neighbor's yard or a few strands of carpet or a splinter of wood from their front door or step. Place the article in a square of black cloth together with the rest of the powder and an egg, upon which you have written the neighbor's name or house address.

Bury the bundle in the earth, well away from your own property. It is said that as the egg rots so too does the satisfaction of the neighbor, for this reason they will be compelled to depart for greener pastures.

A Spell To Protect the Home from Thieves and Intruders

The following spell was offered by a psychic who has had great success with it as have those people she has passed it onto. It calls upon the powerful feminine protective energy of Arachne the ancient Greek spider goddess.

To begin you will need a small amount of spider web. Before taking the web politely ask the spider whose work it is. The web is to be placed in a saucepan of water with a whole ginger root finely grated and a handful of salt. Allow the mixture to come to the boil and then cool.

Decant the cooled mixture into a bottle, retaining a little for use right away. This you must pour into a small cup or dish.

Walk around the entire home both inside and out sprinkling the mixture as you go. While walking, visualize a massive web of protection being woven around the home by an immense spider. See the web as glistening spun steel, growing ever stronger as it is woven and lashed together time and time again.

When you are ready, sit quietly within the home with closed eyes. Again visualize the web, this time as an impenetrable barrier. Atop the web visualize Arachne as a giant spider ready to pounce on thieves and intruders intent on entering your home. Arachne will also catch and eat negative energies directed towards the home.

Each time you leave the home, briefly visualize the spider and her web. Tell her you will be away from the home for a while and you need her to be especially vigilant.

A spider in your home should be considered a blessing. To kill a spider creates a terrible run of bad luck and this should be avoided at all costs. Obviously a toxic spider should not be allowed to roam about the home and it is acceptable to take measures against such a threat.

Magical Aromatherapy for the Home

Using the pure essential oils carefully extracted from flowers and herbs can be a powerful method of therapy but it can also be a very effective magical tool. Below is a list of recipes for use in an oil burner, which may be used to create an atmosphere suited to spells, meditations and visualizations or to enchant the home.

✿ Love Blend (to draw a lover into one's life or to enhance an existing relationship) — one part rose geranium oil, one half part lavender, one part gardenia or ylang ylang. Add a few rose or geranium petals to the water bowl.

✿ Romance Blend (perfect for use in the bedroom or during love spells) — one part cinnamon, one quarter part clove, two parts orange, one part patchouli. Add a piece of fresh root ginger to the water bowl.

✿ Protection Blend (during protection spells, rituals and when feeling threatened) — one part cedarwood, two.parts sandalwood, one half part clove. Add four peppercorns to the water bowl. Optional are a few threads from a spider web which can be added to strengthen the blend.

✿ Psychic Blend (before and during spiritual and psychic work) — one part frankincense, one part sandalwood. Add a few saffron threads to the water bowl.

✿ Angel Blend (for peace and tranquillity or to draw spiritual aid) — one part violet, hyacinth or narcissus, one part chamomile or lavender. Add a piece of angelica or lotus root or white rose petals to the water bowl.

✿ Prosperity Blend (during prosperity spells or to draw wealth to the home) — one part peppermint, one part basil, one half part bergamot. Add five small coins to the water bowl.

✿ Luck and Success Blend (during spells or to draw the energies of luck and success) — one quarter part citronella, two parts lemongrass, one half part cinnamon. Add a small cinnamon quill to the water bowl.

✿ Purifying Blend (during spells or after an unhappy, unpleasant experience in the home. Also excellent for use when moving into a new home) — one part sage, one part rosemary, one half part clove. Add a pinch of salt to the water bowl.

✿ Grounding Blend (when feeling unsettled, depressed or fearful) — one part vetiver, one part oak moss or pine. Add a pinch of earth or a hematite crystal to the water bowl.

✿ Slumber Blend (before sleep and to inspire prophetic dreams) — one part marjoram or oregano, one part lavender. Add a moonstone crystal to the water bowl.

The Magic of Food

The foods we commonly eat today tend to be so highly processed and chemically engineered as to be almost devoid of even a trace of natural energy.

Such foods may nourish our bodies but do little for our spiritual selves. Many organically grown and sensitively handled crops are now becoming standard in our supermarkets. But there are still many goods that we almost must consume which are devoid of the spiritual essences of wild nature.

The traditional concept of praying over a meal finds its roots in the pagan past and is carried on still in many forms of Christianity and Judaism. The point behind blessing food before it is eaten is to thank the bounty of nature for supplying us with our basic needs. In the old world, the thanks were more heartfelt simply because our ancestors didn't always know if and when their next meal would come.

Though we have more certainty, we can at least bless the food we consume and invite the forces of nature into it to render it fit for both our physical and our spiritual sustenance.

A Method of Blessing and Empowering Prepared Food

When preparing a meal intended to have magical significance, it is most important to be in a calm and restful mood. Enjoy the process and through each stage remind yourself why you are making the meal. The energies of love and enjoyment put into every stage of the production will ensure the food is a powerful magical substance.

Once the food is prepared and sitting before you, close your eyes. Pass your hands over the food and imagine a stream of pure white light imbuing it with brilliance. Recite an improvised prayer asking the spirits of nature to enter and bless the food with love, power and healthfulness. Acknowledge the care and thought that has gone into its creation and be thankful that it is both nourishing and delicious. In time you will become aware of lack of energy or life force in foods not blessed and empowered and the richer taste and enjoyment derived from foods which have.

The Power of Fasting Before a Spell

Fasting or denying oneself particular foods for a set period of time towards a goal or aim is a very powerful method of drawing and controlling a particular energy type. When a specific food is chosen to represent a goal or desire and is purposely omitted from the diet, its absence becomes a potent reminder of your goal, for each time you find yourself craving that food, your mind is brought back to the purpose at hand. As the craving grows over the days, so too does the energy which may be finally released and used to power a spell towards the achievement of the goal at the end of the fast. It is important, however, that you never omit a food essential for normal health.

Magical Herbal Teas

Many of the herbs used in spells are also of great use as herbal teas. Taking the power of an enchanted herb into your body is one of the most powerful ways of working magic with herbs.

Some herbs are highly toxic and for this reason it is wise to buy only those herbs you are already familiar with from cooking or those herbs specifically sold as herbal teas through reputable outlets.

Teas are made by pouring a cup of boiling water over a teaspoon of a powdered herb and allowing it to steep for three to five minutes. The tea is then strained. Place your hand over it and close your eyes while you say a silent improvised chant or prayer asking that the tea bring the desired energy into your life. When the tea has cooled a little, drink it.

To ward off negative energies, try sage tea as it is highly protective. Rosemary, allspice, fennel, nettle, fenugreek and lemongrass also keep negative energies at bay. These same herbs may be added to the bath water when you are being affected by negative energies.

To encourage loving energies, try a mixture of orange rind, rose hip and cinnamon. This makes a delicious love tea especially with a little honey. Other herbs said to draw loving energies are parsley, red clover, tansy, chamomile, jasmine petals and chrysanthemum. Also try placing a copper coin in the teapot as the tea steeps as this is the metal of the planet Venus, the astrological ruler of love and romance.

Herbs for luck and opportunity include allspice, lemongrass, aniseed, lemon, lime, eyebright, and thyme. An almond may also be placed in the teapot to pay homage to the astrological planet Mercury, whose domain is chance.

To draw wealth and abundance, try peppermint, spearmint and garden mint. A mixture of one part ginger, and one eighth parts each of clove and nutmeg are also said to attract the energies of wealth and abundance to you. Other such herbs are basil, dandelion, horehound and sarsaparilla.

For focusing on psychic work and developing magical skills, the following herbs are very effective: nutmeg, marjoram, oregano, borage, catnip and linden lime tree flowers.

For soothing restless vibrations, try rose hip, chamomile, valerian, balm, hawthorn berry and maté.

For courage, especially when feeling threatened, herbs of use include parsley, raspberry leaf, nettle, aniseed and ginger.

Foods of Love

There are a countless number of so-called aphrodisiacs from various cultures believed to enhance the act of making love and to inspire thoughts and feelings of love, and may be offered to a desired guest or shared by lovers.

Dairy Foods All milk-based products including cream, yogurt, ice cream and cheese are suffused with the nurturing properties of mothering for milk carries these vibrations. Milk-based foods may be imbued with loving energies and given to a desired lover or shared by a couple.

Fruits Apricots, apples, pears, peaches, sultanas, raisins, persimmons, pomegranates, melons and cherries are filled with the energies of sexual congress for they are the mode of sexual reproduction for plants. The tomato or "love apple" is considered an aphrodisiac.

Vegetables Because of their phallic shapes, cucumbers and asparagus are believed to promote thoughts of love and sex when eaten. The translation of the Aztec name for avocado is "testicle fruit" and eating it was said to heighten a man's sexual drive.

Seafood Oysters and other shell fish have long been thought of as aphrodisiacs. The goddess Venus was said to have been born of the ocean foam, and her loving energies can be found within the fruits of the sea.

Sweets Cakes, sugar, honey, cinnamon, nutmeg, allspice, gingerbread and shortbread are said to be filled with the energies of love. In days of old, cakes were often baked and imbued with love energies and given to desired men or women.

Chocolate is said to be full of pheromones or sexual hormones and eating vast amounts of this treat is said to make one fall in love easily.

Presentation

When preparing a meal of magical significance for inviting the energies of love into the room, create the right ambience with a tablecloth and candle in colors of vivid red or pink, with a central flower arrangement of red and yellow roses, jasmine, lavender, honeysuckle or violets.

Foods of Prosperity

The energies of prosperity can be found in many foods and a special magical meal may be created using a combination of many of the foods found below.

Grain Prosperous energies are found in all grains, beans and seeds, and special magical breads may be made with a few different types of grains, nuts and herbs under the influence of the planets Mercury, Jupiter and the Sun. Grains and seeds of prosperity include oats, rice, corn or maize, wheat, rye, barley, millet and sesame seeds.

Vegetables All green and leafy vegetables, such as spinach, chard and broccoli contain the essences of the planet Jupiter which is assigned to the realm of prosperity, abundance and expansion.

Yams, sweet potatoes, celeriac, potatoes and other tuberous root vegetables are the staff of life for many cultures around the earth, and to own a number of these is to be considered wealthy and powerful.

Okra or lady finger is a traditional prosperity vegetable which may be eaten on a Thursday, perhaps in a gumbo (the spicy stew from the American South) to draw the blessings of the spirits of prosperity.

Carob is often used as a substitute for chocolate, however in magical lore the seed pods of the carob plant are referred to as St John's Bread, and to carry one is to be blessed with great wealth.

Spices The luxurious spice saffron is taken from the crocus flower and is literally worth its weight in gold. For this reason it is believed to bring vast amounts of prosperity, good fortune and abundance when eaten in a magical meal.

Presentation

A special prosperity meal may be created with a green and gold theme. Perhaps a green table cloth could be combined with golden candles and napkin rings. A luxurious flower arrangement can be made with palm fronds, oak and holly leaves, marigolds, sunflowers and other vivid yellow flowers.

Foods to Promote Protection

We rarely feel vulnerable when we are physically healthy. Often when we are run down things which would normally not bother us can take on a threatening significance. For this reason it is important to eat a very healthy diet when we are feeling vulnerable. The energies of certain foods are considered to be most beneficial at these times. These are listed below:

Vegetables Carrots, capsicum or peppers, garlic, ginger, artichokes, cabbage, onions, shallots, spring onions and leeks are said to surround the user in the energies of protection when consumed regularly.

Fruits Blueberry, pineapple, grapefruit, coconut, lemon, citron and bananas carry strong protective energies which will be released by being eaten and taken into the body.

Herbs and Spices Many hot and spicy foods are said to be protective especially those made with chilli, tarragon, fennel, bay laurel leaves, lemongrass, garlic, ginger, mustard and peppercorns.

Coffee and Tea These widely consumed beverages are said to surround the user in strong vibrations from the planet Mars which help build up courage and fortitude.

Meats Beef is believed to give the consumer the vibrations of courage and strength, especially when cooked with some of the herbs and spices mentioned above.

Salt Although for health reasons many of us are concerned with the amount of salt in our diets a little of this much abused mineral is beneficial when in need of a little extra protection.

Presentation

For an appropriate table layout for a meal intended to draw the energies of protection, choose a grey, black or white table cloth, grey candles and a flower arrangement consisting of gardenias, marigolds, rosemary and lavender.

Foods of Luck and Success

The energies of luck, success and prosperity can be found in many foods and a special magical meal may be created using a combination of many of the foods found below.

Nuts The energies of luck can be found in abundance in various types of nuts under the astrological persuasion of the planet Mercury. Such nuts include hazel, almond, walnut, pecan, Brazil, peanuts, chestnuts.

Fruits and Vegetables Mushrooms are considered very lucky when eaten after a wish has been made over them. Artichokes, both the globe and Jerusalem varieties, have light, airy and Mercurial vibrations well suited to a magical meal for promoting success and luck. A grapefruit sweetened with honey and eaten once a week is said to draw the energies of success. Citron, kumquat and quince are all associated with the magic of success.

Beans A special dish of spicy red beans cooked with cayenne pepper and garlic is said to draw bounty to the home when eaten.

Eggs A magically enchanted egg which when eaten is believed to bring luck is simply made by being boiled in water to which yellow food dye and cinnamon powder has been added. The egg is allowed to cool and a secret wish for luck and success is made over it before being eaten.

Spices Ginger and lemongrass are believed to invite the blessings of the capricious spirits of chance and luck.

Presentation
Choose a vivid yellow, orange or golden table cloth, yellow candles and a flower arrangement consisting of orange and yellow flowers and perhaps even fruits for a magical meal to court the favor of the spirits of luck and success.

The World

The magical concept of the world as a mirror of the self is a very ancient one and within this concept lies the value of individual action towards peace and love within the world as a whole. For the world to reflect the kinds of values so many of us hold we must be willing to express love for all the life forms with which we share this planet.

In ancient times the natural world was wild and untamed, humanity looked upon the ebb and flow of the seasons, the cycles of the moon and planets and the ever-present sun as divine forces without which we could not survive. In cathedrals of trees and groves, the natural world was worshiped. Humanity felt a connection to the earth, the planets, seas and heavens, and within the world of our ancestors there was both meaning and mystery in all things. Animals and plants shared the earth with humanity both as sources of food and as totem spirits. Everywhere there was balance.

Since the industrial revolution the quest of humanity has been to overpower and dominate nature. We have come to view all other life forms, plants and animals as existing solely for our human needs. We have seized and subjugated the seas, the kingdoms of the animals and plants, yet everywhere we see the ruin we are causing.

Slowly the tide is turning as we come to understand that nature will not be dominated by humanity, it will only die under our control.

In the following section magic for world peace and the protection of the environment can be found as can the magic of world travel.

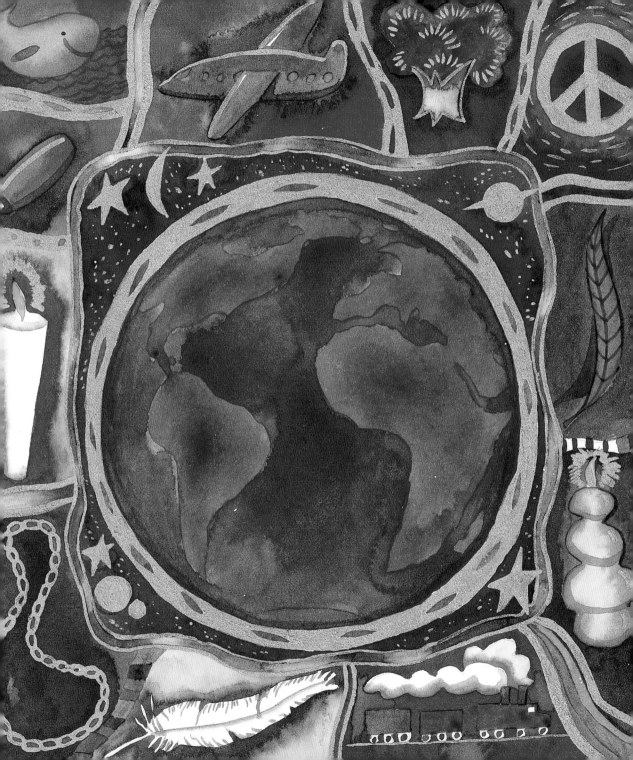

A Spell for World Peace and a Pure World Environment

The following spell is a method of tapping into the stream of universal peace energy and making your own little piece of the world brighter by nullifying negative energy.

You will need the following items:

✡ *a white candle (peace)*
✡ *a white feather (peace)*
✡ *a green leaf (environment)*
✡ *a blue bead or marble (the world)*
✡ *a small jar of spring water sweetened with sugar*

Light the candle, extinguish any artificial illumination and arrange all items before you. Sit for a moment and still the mind. Focus on the candle flame and recall the images that represent war, see in your mind's eye the steady destruction of the natural world. Close your eyes and breathe deeply to rid yourself of these images.

See how a chain of fearful acts can quickly degenerate into violence. Refuse to participate in this cycle of anger and fear as it may stop with you if you are willing to earth the energy by breathing it out.

Hold the marble or bead in your hand and feel the fragility of the earth in the hands of humanity, feel the destructive potential of greed and fear. Blow a cool stream of breath upon the bead or marble. Take up the white feather and dip it into the water. Using the feather as a paintbrush bathe the marble or bead; take up the leaf and do the same. Place the bead or marble into the jar of water and visualize the world spinning slowly in a bank of beautiful billowing clouds. Place the jar in a cool quiet part of the home where it will not be disturbed. Put the feather beneath your bed and allow the candle to burn out by itself.

Here the spell ends but the true work begins. In your daily life practice the art of releasing and ending a cycle of fear and malice and also do your own small part toward the end of environmental destruction.

A Spell for Safety in World Travel

The world has become a very small place in these days of swift international travel. However, so often we are troubled by concerns about a loved one while overseas. The spell below is a method of protecting a traveler while away from home and it may either be performed by the self for the self or on behalf of a loved one about to take a trip.

You will need the following items:

✡ *an orange candle*
✡ *a length of fine thread copper wire (as long as your arm)*
✡ *a blue bead*
✡ *a neck chain or a length of leather strip*
✡ *lavender, sandalwood or lemongrass incense*

The spell is to be performed on a Wednesday early in the morning, at dawn if possible. The candle and other items should be neatly placed before you. The blue bead must have an opening large enough through which to thread the chain or leather strip; this will become an amulet to be worn by the traveler.

Coil the copper wire around the candle from the base to the tip, creating a spiral design. The candle and incense can now be lit.

Holding the chain (or leather) and bead in hand recite the following:

"Little King Mercury, swift and alert, be on guard here and watch ever vigilantly for me (or name of traveler). Bless this amulet made in your name and let it be a stout and true guard against all malady, hurt, fear, trial and tribulation."

Breathe upon the amulet seventeen times with your eyes closed and feel the energy of your breath grow stronger and more potent with each breath. Attempt to push the energy into the amulet. If desired the amulet may be anointed with lemongrass essential oil before being worn by the traveler.

First published by Lansdowne Publishing Pty Ltd, 1997
This edition published in 1998 by

Parkgate Books
Kiln House
210 New King's Road
London SW6 4NZ
Great Britain

1 3 5 7 9 8 6 4 2

REPRINTED 1999

British Library Cataloguing in Publication Data:
A catalogue record for this book is available from the British Library

ISBN 1 85585 512 7

Publisher: Deborah Nixon
Production Manager: Sally Stokes
Project Co-ordinator: Jenny Coren
Illustrators: Joanna Davies, Sue Ninham
Editor: Cynthia Blanche
Designer: Sylvie Abecassis
Layouts: Stephanie Doyle

Set in Cochin on QuarkXpress
Printed in Singapore by Tien Wah Press (Pte) Ltd